Mel Bay Presents
FAVORITE HYMNS
FOR PIANO SOLO
by Tim Price

Favorite Hymns for Piano Solo is a collection of favorite hymns carefully arranged by Tim Price for solo piano. Mr. Price had delved into the treasury of Christian music through the ages and selected hymns which have been used and loved by all denominations of the Christian faith. The arrangements vary in style and are new and fresh approaches to these well-known hymns. It is with pleasure that we present this book for personal and group worship and praise.

Free audio available online!
Visit: www.melbay.com/freedownload/

© 2008, 1978 BY MEL BAY PUBLICATIONS, INC., PACIFIC, MO 63069.
ALL RIGHTS RESERVED. INTERNATIONAL COPYRIGHT SECURED. B.M.I. MADE AND PRINTED IN U.S.A.
No part of this publication may be reproduced in whole or in part, or stored in a retrieval system, or transmitted in any form or by any means, electronic, mechanical, photocopy, recording, or otherwise, without written permission of the publisher.

Visit us on the Web at www.melbay.com — E-mail us at email@melbay.com

Contents

All Creatures of Our God and King 27

American Folk Hymn 15

Breathe on Me, Breath of God 6

Come Thou Almighty King 11

Come, Thou Long Expected Jesus 3

Jesus, the Very Thought of Thee 30

Lead, Kindly Light 18

Let All Mortal Flesh Keep Silence 8

Rock of Ages 24

True Happiness 21

COME, THOU LONG EXPECTED JESUS

Original melody by ROWLAND H. PRICHARD
arr. by Tim Price

NOTES

This old Advent hymn, originally known as "Hyfrydol", is one of the more well-known in Christian hymn literature. Here, it is given a thoughtful, modal setting.

BREATHE ON ME, BREATH OF GOD

by ROBERT JACKSON
arr. by Tim Price

NOTES

This quiet and simple melody gives expression to the Christian's hope for the Holy Spirit to live within his life, and is usually heard during the season of Pentecost.

LET ALL MORTAL FLESH KEEP SILENCE

TRAD. FRENCH TUNE
arr. by Tim Price

NOTES

This haunting melody, also known as "Picardy," represents the darkness before the light, the longing anticipation of the coming of the Christ into the world. The passage in 3/4 at the beginning should accentuate the mood of the piece.

COME THOU ALMIGHTY KING

FELICE DE GIARDINI
arr. by Tim Price

Slower to the end.

NOTES
This triumphant call to worship is given two contrasting settings in this arrangement. The performer should carefully observe changes in tempo as indicated.

AMERICAN FOLK HYMN

arr. by Tim Price

NOTES
Though the middle section of this piece is rather bold and complex, an over-all sensitivity and simplicity should be maintained in this beautiful song, an outgrowth of American Christian music about the turn of the last century.

LEAD, KINDLY LIGHT

by JOHN B. DYKES
arr. by Tim Price

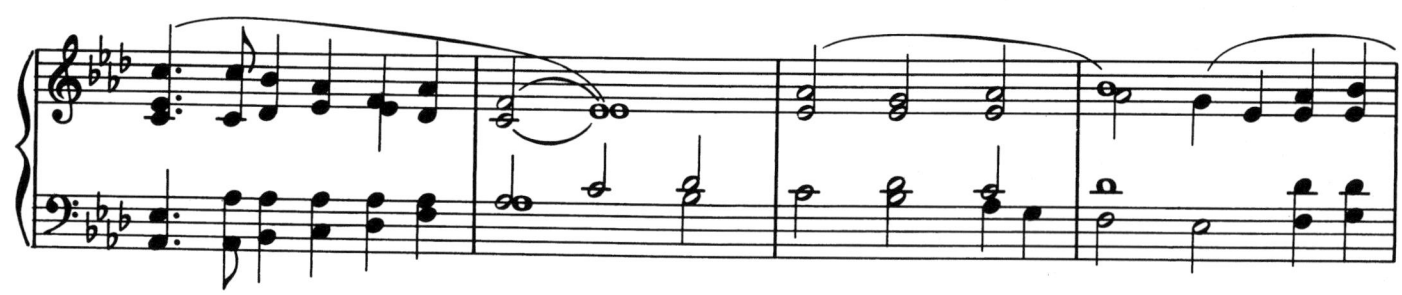
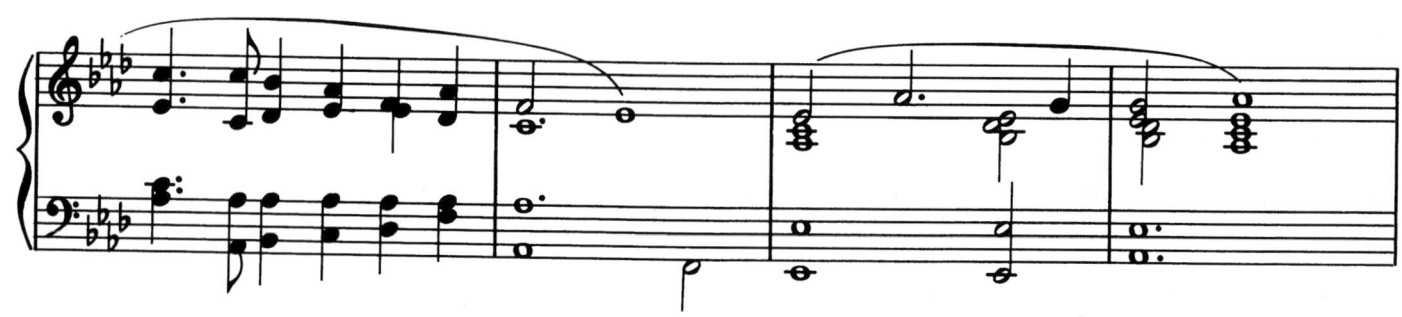

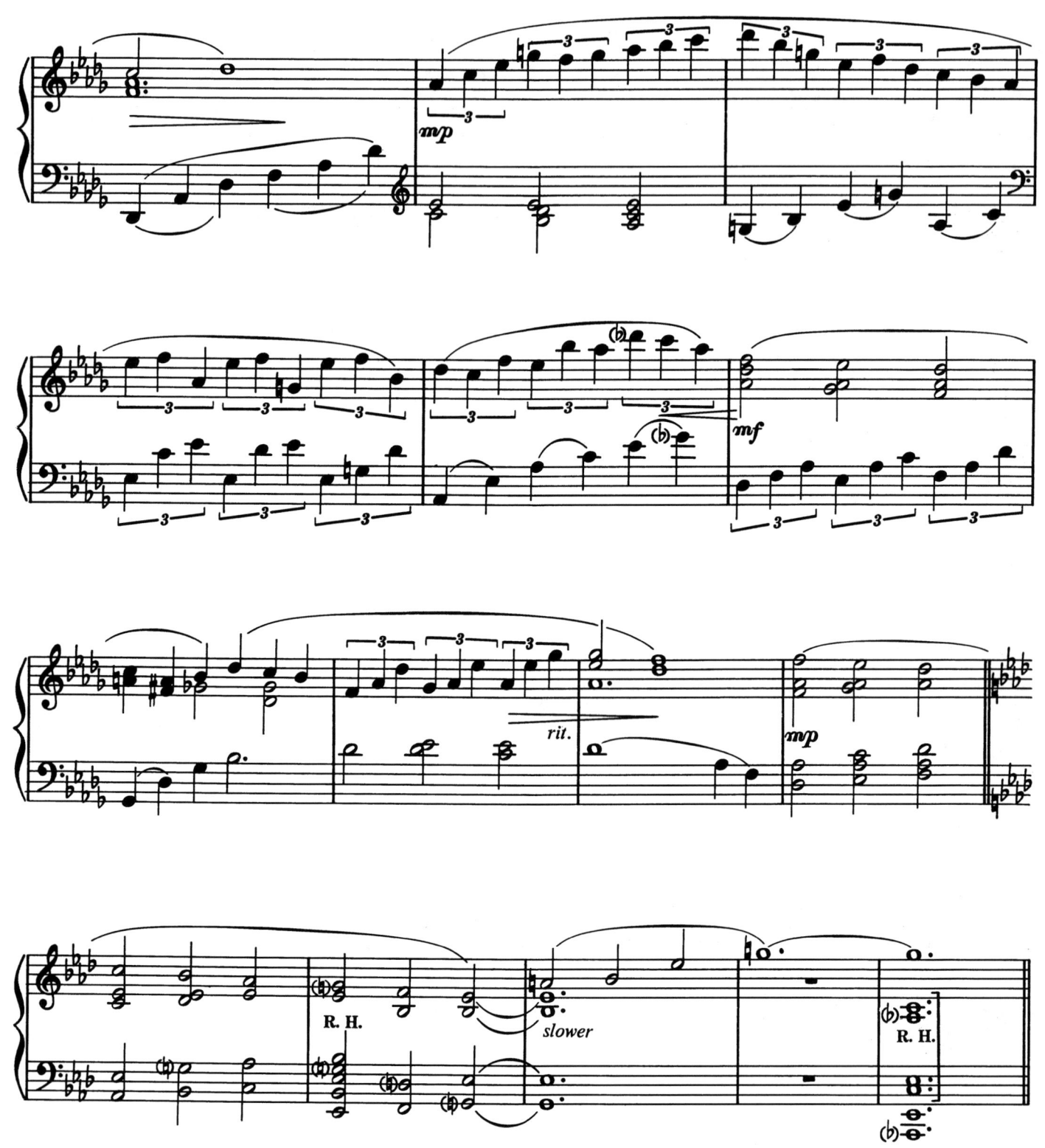

NOTES

This beautiful hymn of prayer dates from the middle 1800's. The performer should always be careful not to let the triplet accompaniment figures dominate the melody in the middle section of the arrangement.

TRUE HAPPINESS

From "SOUTHERN HARMONY," 1835
arr. by Tim Price

NOTES

Though not indicated by the title (also known as "How Happy Are They"), the arranger has felt the best setting for this piece to be one of quiet mysterious strength; the image of its origins in the mountains of Appalachia.

ROCK OF AGES

by THOMAS HASTINGS
arr. by Tim Price

NOTES

This hymn is one of the most familiar to American Christians. Play it in a peaceful, straight forward manner.

ALL CREATURES OF OUR GOD AND KING

From "GEISTLICHE KIRCHENGESANGE"
arr. by Tim Price

NOTES

Strength, strict tempo and decisive articulation are the bywords for performance of this well-known hymn-tune.

JESUS, THE VERY THOUGHT OF THEE

by JOHN B. DYKES
arr. by Tim Price

NOTES

The elegant composition of this tune allows it to easily assume a classical style. Therefore, play it as you would a piece by Schumann or Brahms.